AF349112

13
called    her    Wuzz  -  y,    be  -  cause    she    was    like
5                                                              1


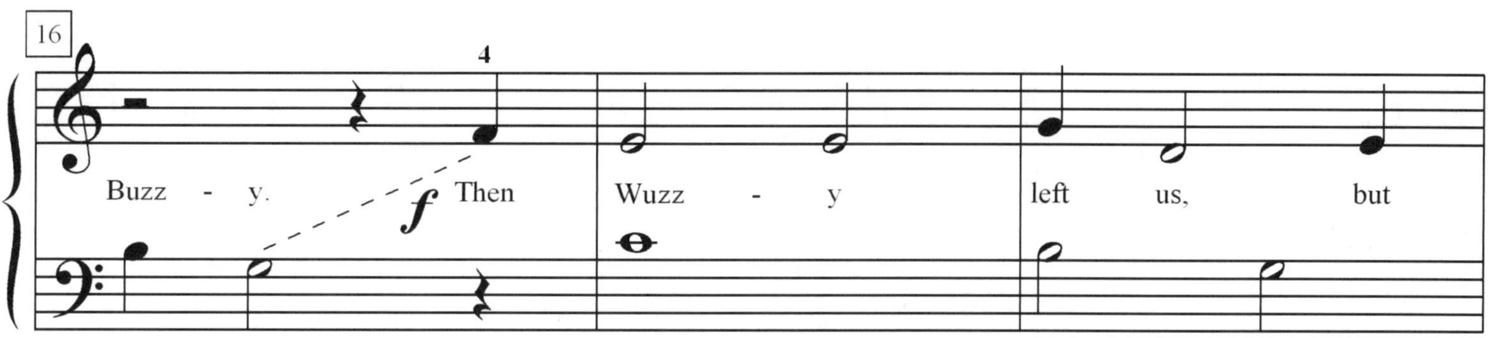

16
Buzz  -  y.    f    Then    Wuzz  -  y    left    us,    but
4

19
Buzz  -  y    said    she'd    stay.    She    said    "Me  -


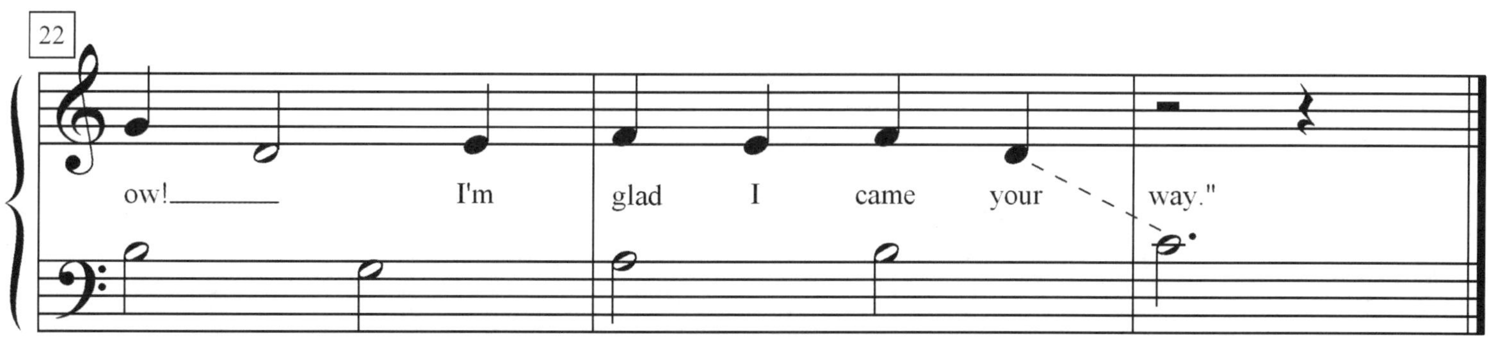

22
ow!_______    I'm    glad    I    came    your    way."

# Kangaroo Hop

Giocoso ♩ = 116-126

Mary Ann Polk

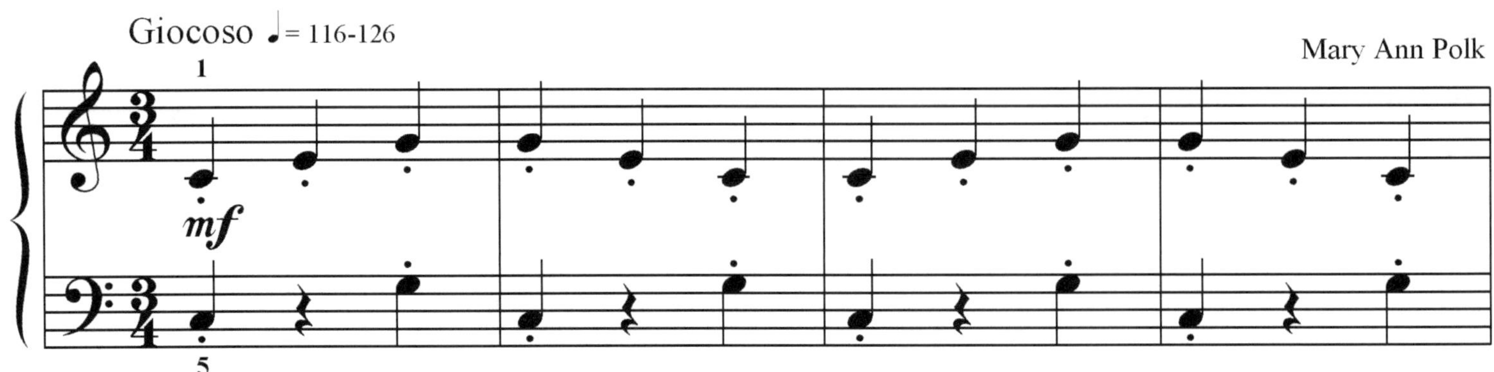

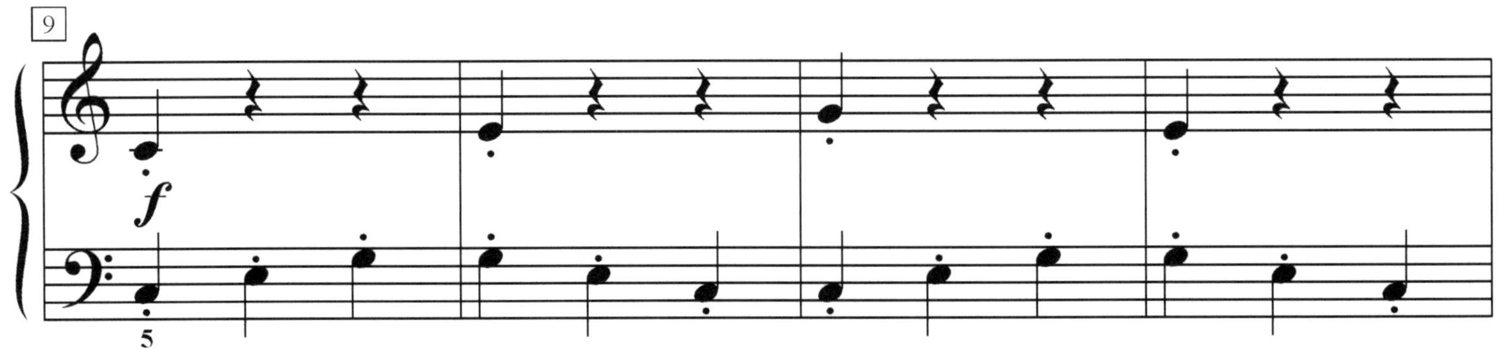

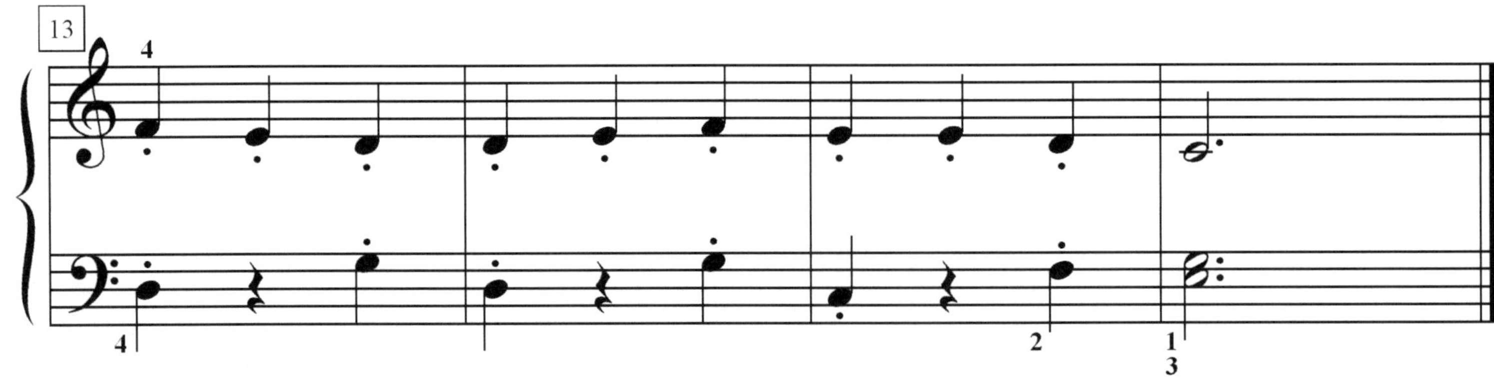

# The Elephant

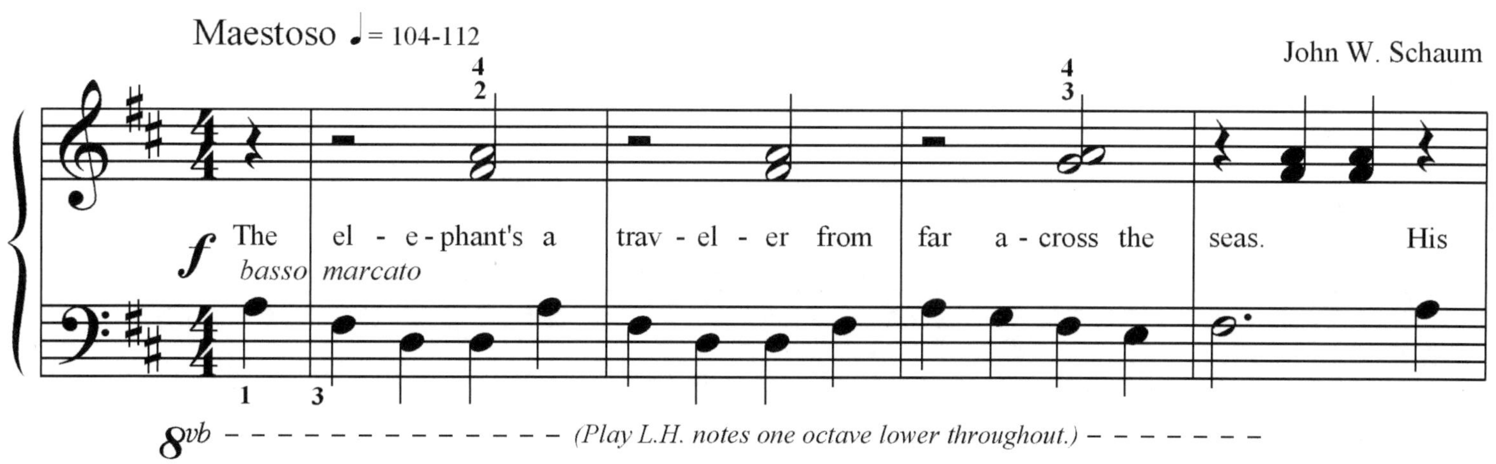

Maestoso ♩ = 104-112
John W. Schaum
f
basso marcato
The el - e - phant's a trav - el - er from far a - cross the seas. His
8vb (Play L.H. notes one octave lower throughout.)

cir - cus acts are fun to watch. He real - ly likes to please. He
mp

al - so has a room - y trunk to take where - e'er he goes. He
ff

gets re - wards and treats ga - lore for fun - ny tricks he knows.

# Puppy Love

Moderato ♩ = 112-120

Susan Sprengeler

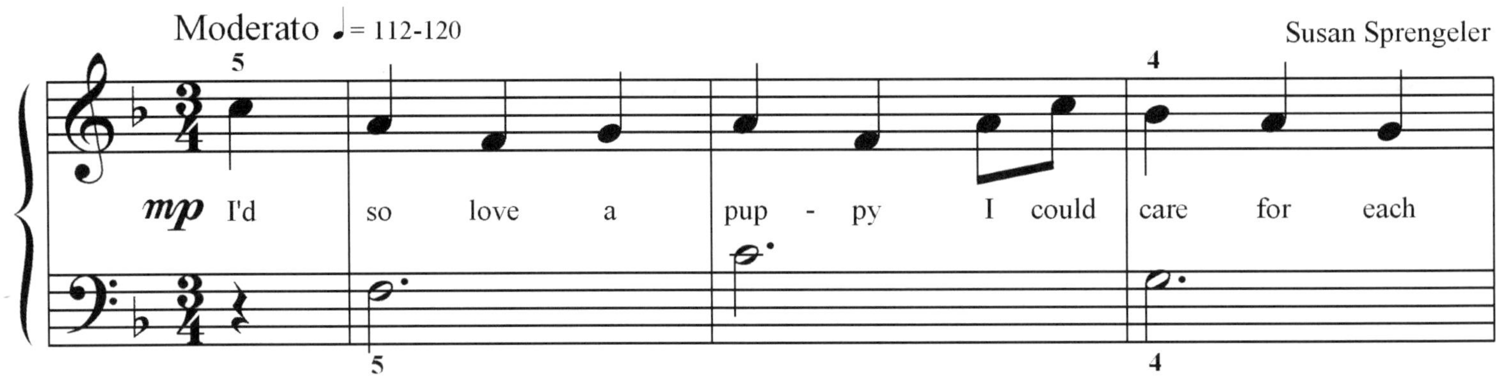

mp I'd so love a pup - py I could care for each

day. He'd make me so hap - py in his

own spe - cial way. I'd feed him and
mf

comb him, he'd romp all a - round. And

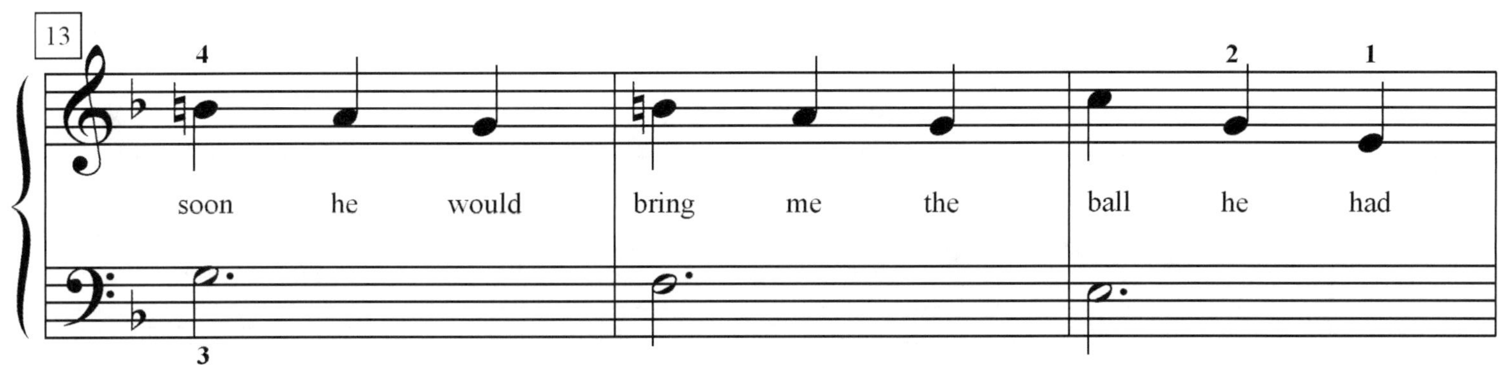
13
4
2   1
soon   he   would   bring   me   the   ball   he   had
3

16
5
found!   I'd   treat   him   so   well   that   he   would
mp
1   5

19
4
not   run   a - way.   I'd   so   love   a
mf

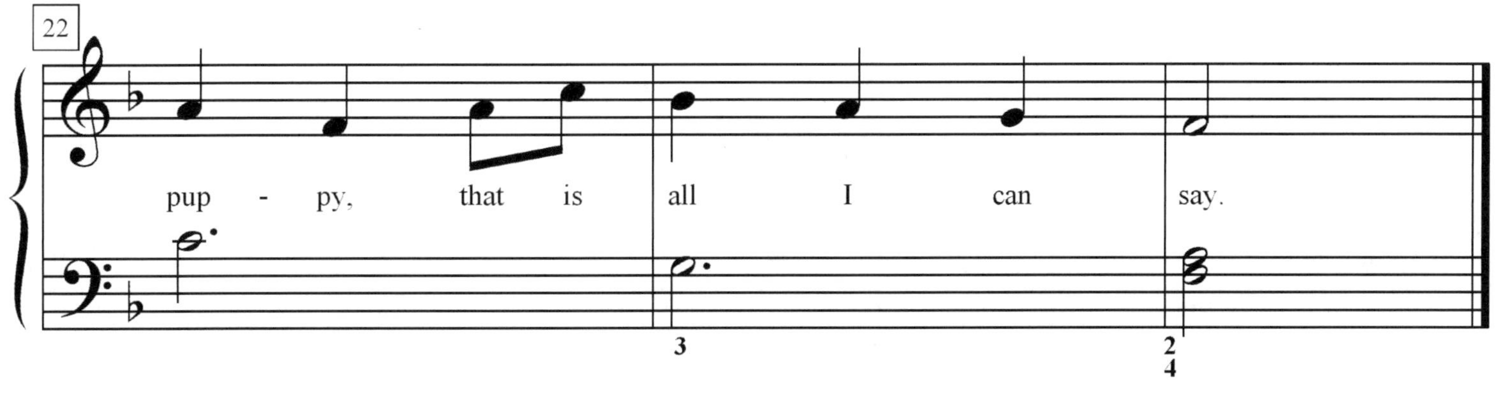
22
pup - py,   that   is   all   I   can   say.
3   2
4

# Playful Poodle

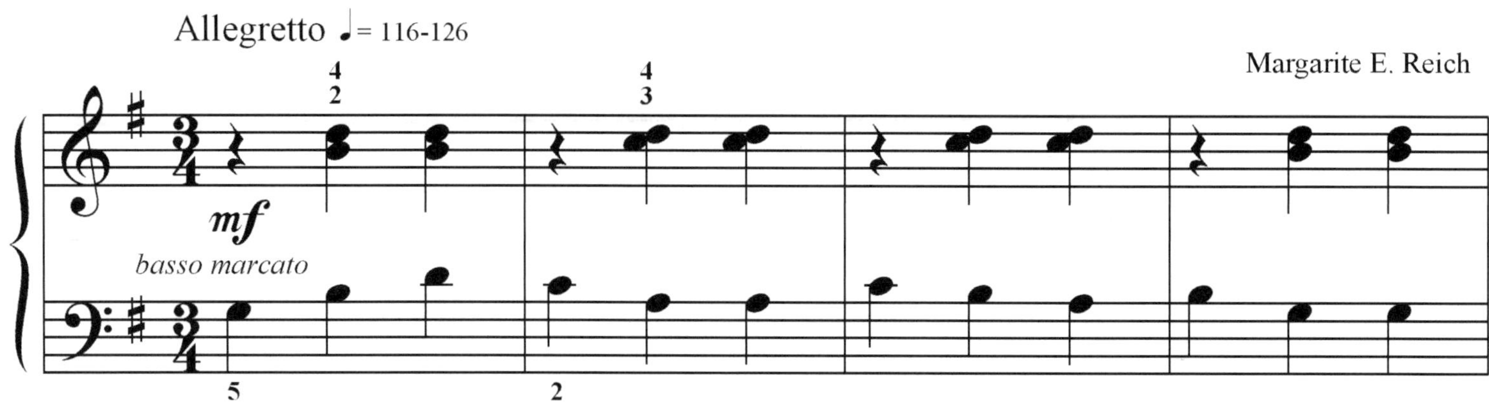


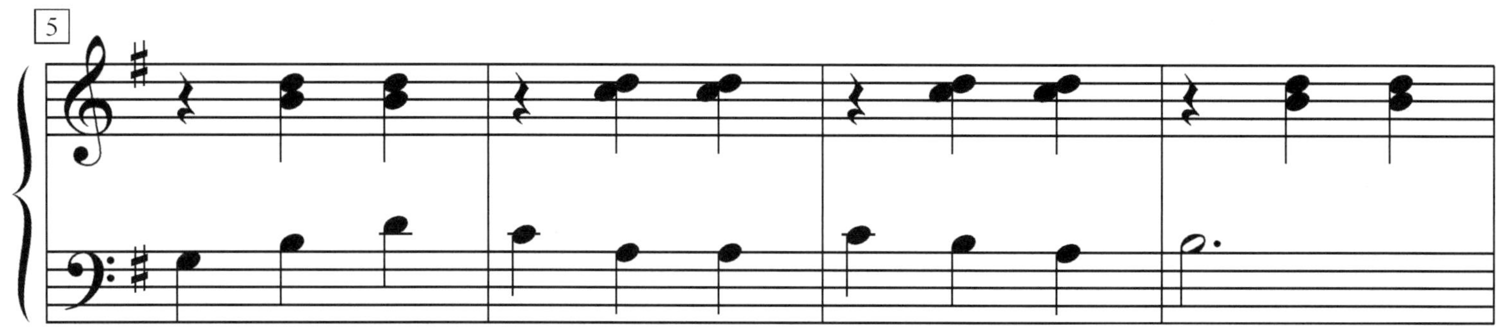

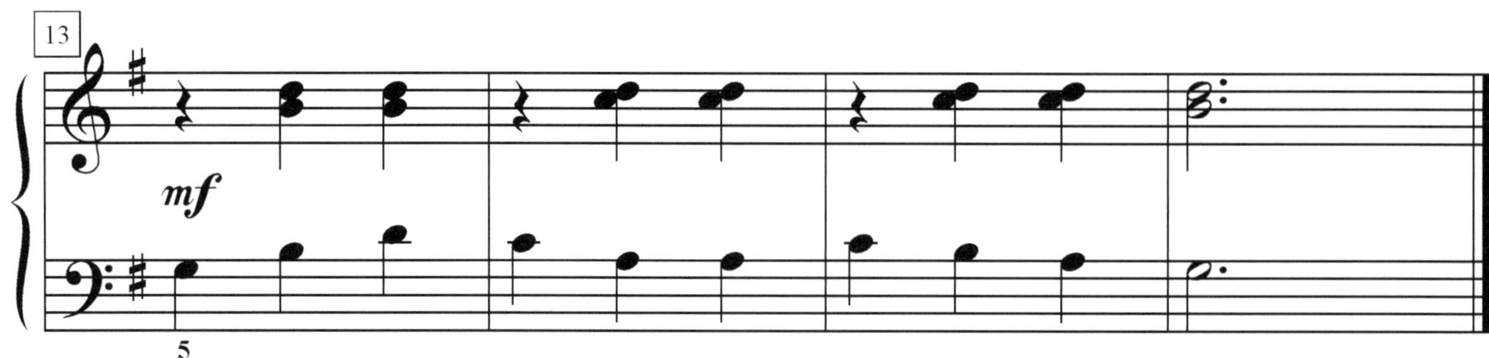

# The Cuckoo and the Parakeet

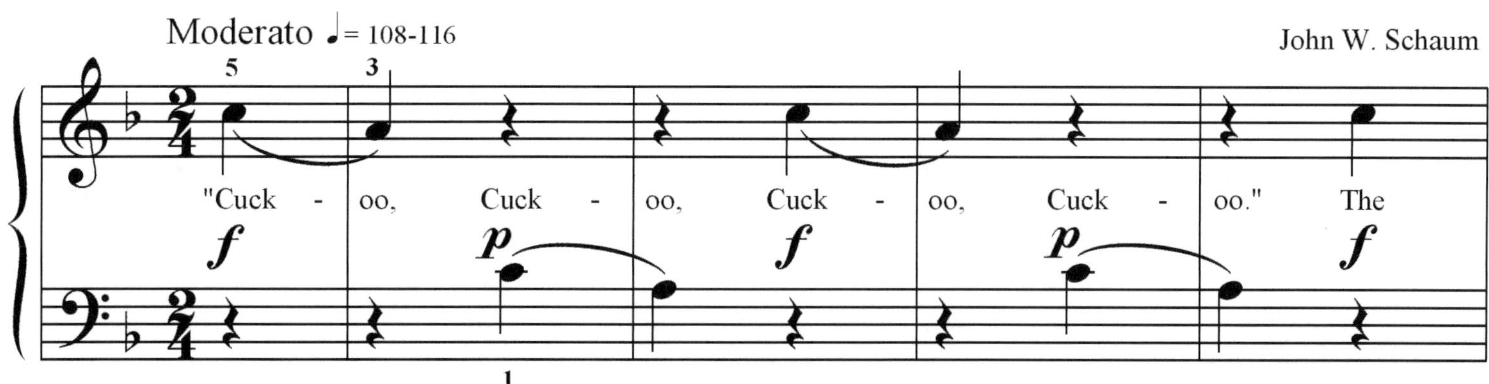

Moderato ♩ = 108-116
John W. Schaum
"Cuck - oo, Cuck - oo, Cuck - oo, Cuck - oo." The
f p f p f

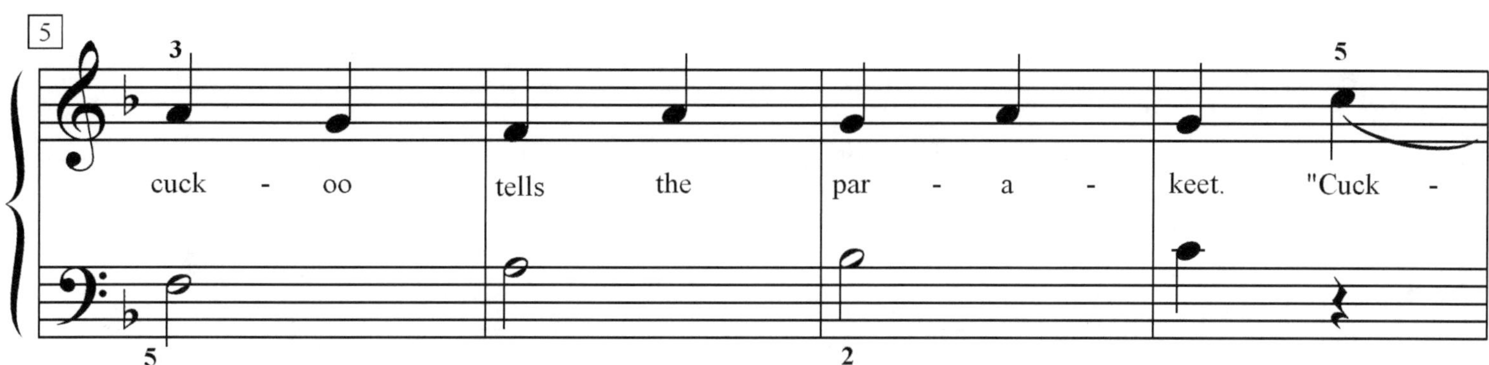

cuck - oo tells the par - a - keet. "Cuck -

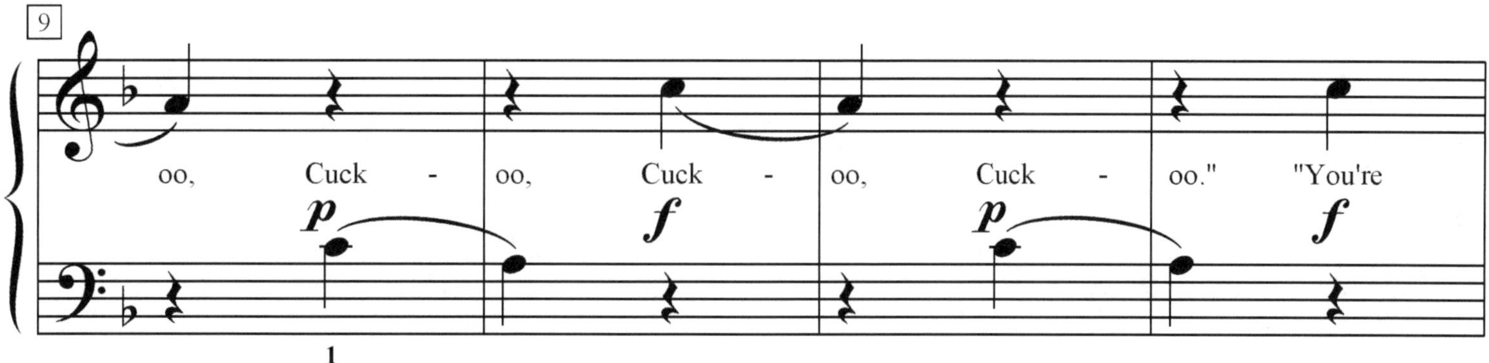

oo, Cuck - oo, Cuck - oo, Cuck - oo." "You're
p f p f

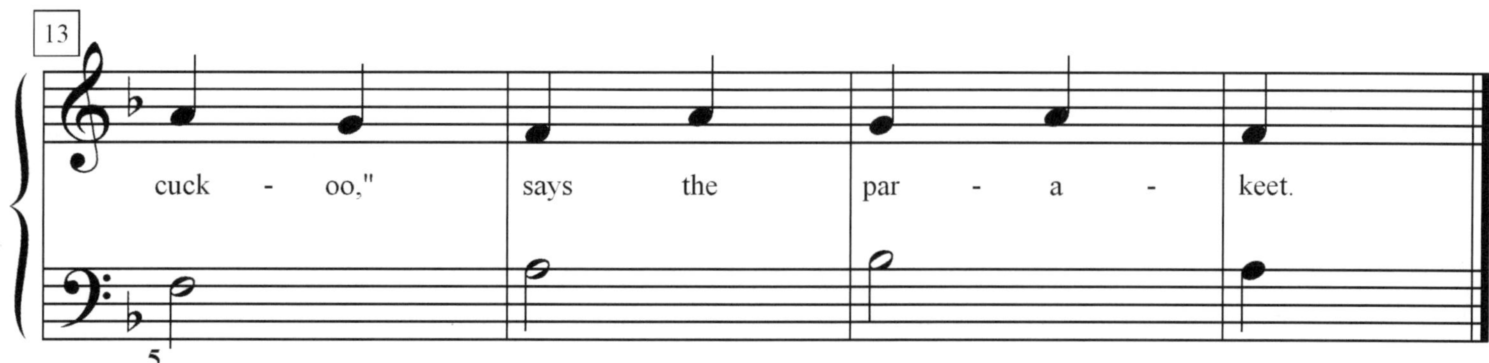

cuck - oo," says the par - a - keet.

# Penguins at Play

Julia Heim
*Lyrics by John W. Schaum*

Moderato ♩ = 116-120
mf Pen - guins at play, Ant - arc - tic bay.

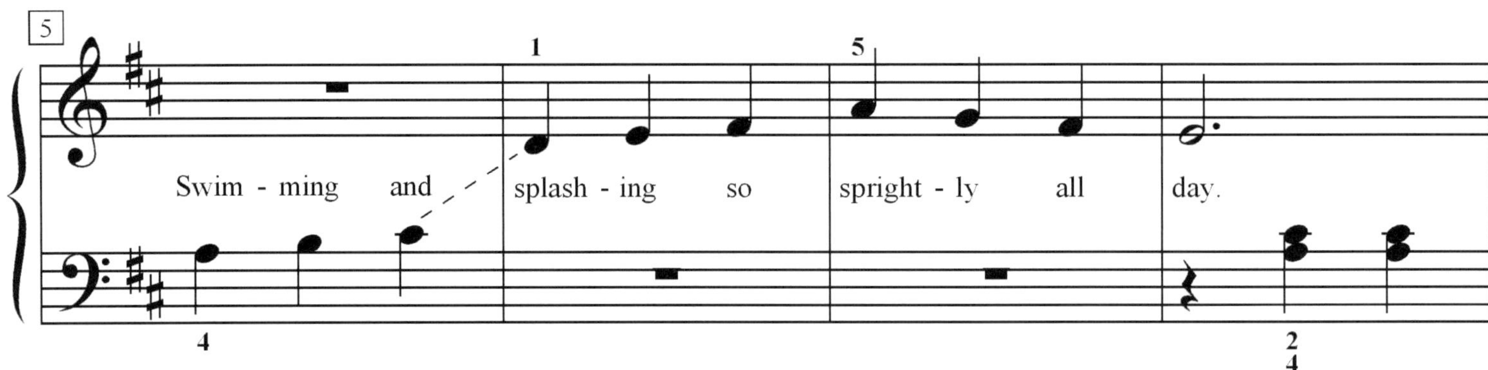

Swim - ming and splash - ing so spright - ly all day.

f Pen - guins are trim, birds neat and prim.

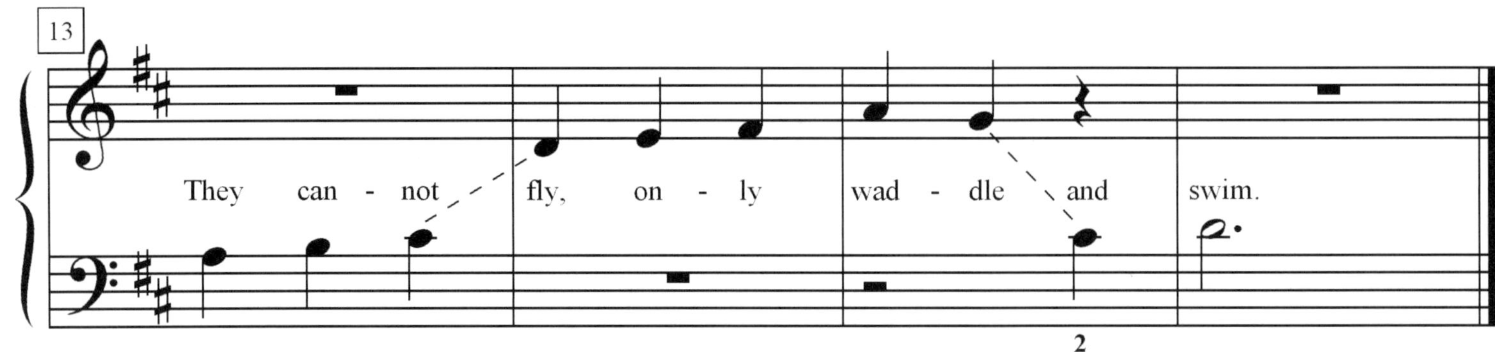

They can - not fly, on - ly wad - dle and swim.